CHRIS EVERT LLOYD
WOMEN'S TENNIS CHAMPION

BRACEVILLE SCHOOL LIBRARY

By Dorothy Childers Schmitz

Reprinted 1978, 1980

Library of Congress Catalog Card Number: 77-70891. International Standard Book Number: 0-913940-64-X.

Design - Doris Woods and Randal M. Heise

PHOTOGRAPHIC CREDITS

A little girl watches her father play tennis. She likes to watch the game. She wants to play, too.

The next day her father takes her onto the court with him. He throws out a few balls for her to hit. She misses them all. But her father knows that she will learn. How does this little girl grow up to be one of the best women tennis players in all the world? This is her story.

Chris Evert at the age of seventeen with her family: John, Mrs. Evert, Jeanne, Mr. Evert, Drew, and Clare.

Christine Marie Evert was born into a family of tennis players. They lived in Fort Lauderdale, Florida. Their house was near the tennis courts where Mr. Evert gave tennis lessons.

Chris had two brothers and two sisters. They all loved to play tennis. But it was Chris who seemed to work harder than the others. By the time she was seven, she was working at her game for four hours every day of the week. On weekends she was practicing nine hours a day.

Chris practices every day after school.

All this hard work began to show. When she was eight years old, she won a trophy with another player. They were runners-up in an Orange Bowl doubles tournament. By the time she was eleven, she had reached a national standing.

After school, Chris and her younger sister Jeanne would go straight to the court for practice. Chris was willing to practice for hours. Even when it was time to go, she would say, "Just let me hit a few more."

Chris became more and more interested in tennis. Her father could see that she was getting better and better. But he could see her weaknesses, too. One of her weaknesses was her backhand. He taught her to hold the racket with both hands for backhand shots. This worked so well for her that she became known for her unusual backhand.

At fourteen, Chris wins her first junior championship.

All the hard work paid off for Chris. When she was fourteen, she won the national championship for fourteen-year-old girls.

As Chris became better known, she played in more and more tournaments. By the time she was fifteen, she was playing older women who had played in many more tournaments than she had. In 1970, she beat Francoise Durr of France and Margaret Court, a Wimbledon champion!

Chris never stopped practicing. Winning did not make her think that she was as good as she could be. She still wanted to play better. She worked hard. All the time she was practicing hard, she was earning good grades. She was a student at St. Thomas Aquinas Catholic High School. She practiced and studied, too. So she did not have time to do many of the things her friends did. There were no slumber parties for her. She was too busy.

Chris joins her classmates at St. Thomas Aquinas High School.

In 1971, Chris had a chance to play a really famous player - Billie Jean King. They played in the Virginia Slims Masters Tournament. Chris won! That same year she won the Girls' 18 and the Orange Bowl.

After these victories, Chris was invited to play in a very important tournament. It was called the U.S. Wightman Cup Team. It was a contest between the United States and England.

It was a very important contest. Many people said she was too young for a contest like this. But she played so well that she made it to the finals! Everyone was asking, "Can Chris Evert bring home the Wightman Cup for the U.S.? Can she beat the best woman player in England?" She did it! She beat Virginia Wade 6-1, 6-1.

Chris accepts congratulations from Francoise Durr at Forest Hills.

Chris went to the U.S. Open in 1971. This was a very important tournament in Forest Hills, New York. She beat Edda Budding of Germany. Her next opponent was Mary Ann Eisel. Chris won again. Then Chris played a match with Francoise Durr. The crowd became very excited. When Chris won again, they stood up and cheered.

Chris defeats Lesley Hunt at Forest Hills.

Lesley Hunt from Australia was her next opponent. Miss Hunt won the first set. But Chris won the next two sets, and the match. Chris Evert was the youngest woman ever to reach the semi-finals at Forest Hills.

17

The next match was with Billie Jean King. Billie Jean won at Wimbledon three times. She defeated Chris again 6-3, 6-2. So Chris did not get to the finals. But people had seen enough to know that Chris Evert would be back again.

Chris became well-known after her tournament at Forest Hills. Sports writers were calling her the most exciting young tennis star in America. Some of them began to call her "Little Miss Sunshine." She wore pigtails and pretty tennis dresses. More and more people came to watch her play. She had made her hometown famous. Her classmates and friends were proud of her.

Chris's parents wanted to keep her free from too much news about her. They still wanted her to study and practice. They wanted her to live the same kind of life she always did. They did not want her to change in any way. So Chris continued to work hard. She kept a better than B average even with all she had to do. There were many hours of practice. She had to travel to and from tournaments. Still she was an honor roll student. She was even chosen for the National Honor Society.

People noticed that Chris was always polite. She was even shy at times. She said, "I don't really enjoy all the fuss made over me."

But she did enjoy playing tennis. "I can't say the practice is fun," she said, "But the tournaments are. I love the perfection part . . . I'm going to turn pro as soon as I can."

The next tournament was the Women's International Tournament. Chris had to play Billie Jean King again. This time, Chris won! Then she was ready for Wimbledon. At Wimbledon, Chris made it to the semi-finals. So did a young star from Australia. Her name was Evonne Goolagong. The crowd was really excited about this match. Here were two young stars. They wanted to see which one was better. Chris won the first set, 6-4. Evonne won the second, 6-3. When Evonne won again, 6-4, Chris was defeated. But she was not discouraged. She had played well. Evonne had played even better. Chris looked forward to her next chance to play Evonne.

Evonne Goolagong and Chris meet at the net after their Wimbledon match.

That chance came soon. In the spring of 1972, Chris defeated Evonne in the Bonne Bell Cup Matches. Chris took home the Bonne Bell Cup for the U.S.

In August of that same year, Chris defeated Evonne again. This time it was the National Clay Courts Tournament. It was Chris Evert's first Clay Courts title. But it would not be her last.

In the fall of 1972, Chris went back to Forest Hills. Again she made it to the semifinals. But she lost to Kerry Melville, 6-4, 6-2. She had lost at Forest Hills again. But she did not give up.

By this time, Chris was known everywhere. Many reporters wanted to write about her. They asked her all kinds of questions. She still did not want people to make a big fuss over her. "I'm just a seventeen-year-old girl who loves tennis," she said.

Sometimes she was nervous about the interviews. She thought they were harder than playing the tournaments. Once she was telling friends about an interview. She said, "I opened my mouth and nothing came out!"

CHRIS EVERT LLOYD

WOMEN'S TENNIS CHAMPION